Big

Toddler

Coloring Book

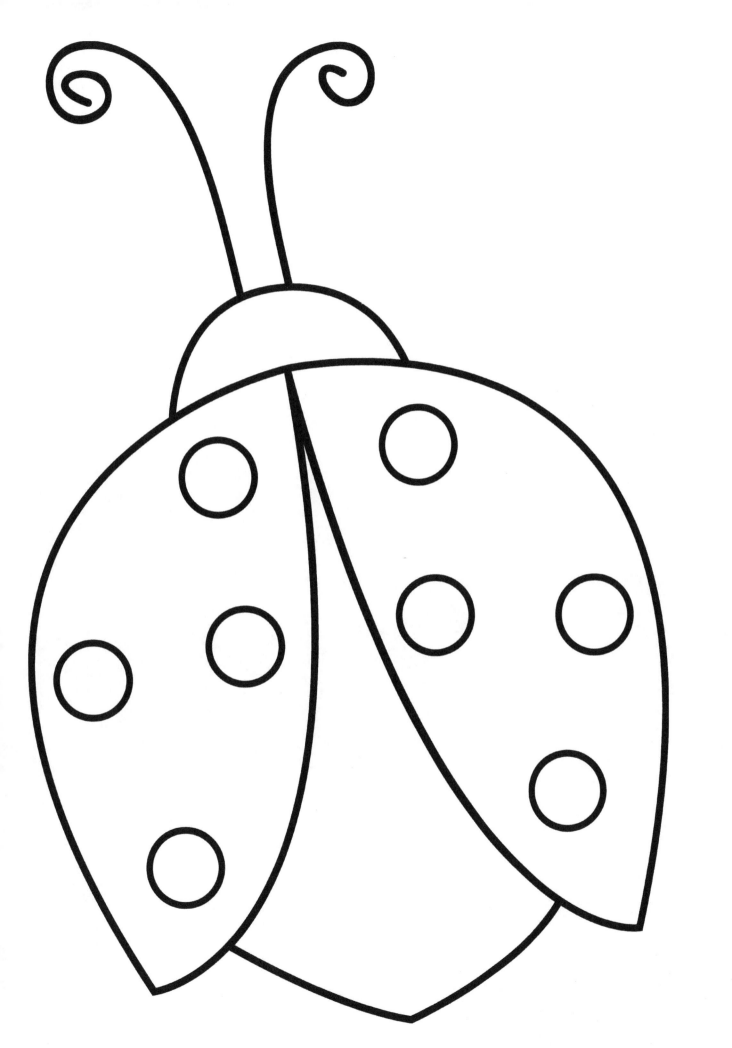

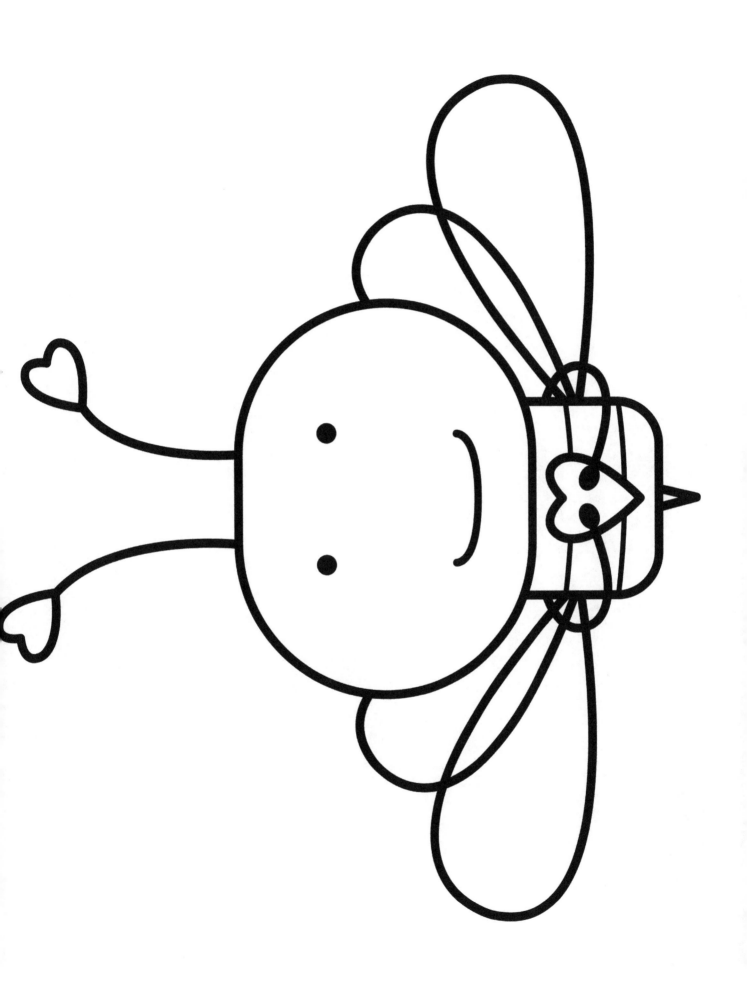

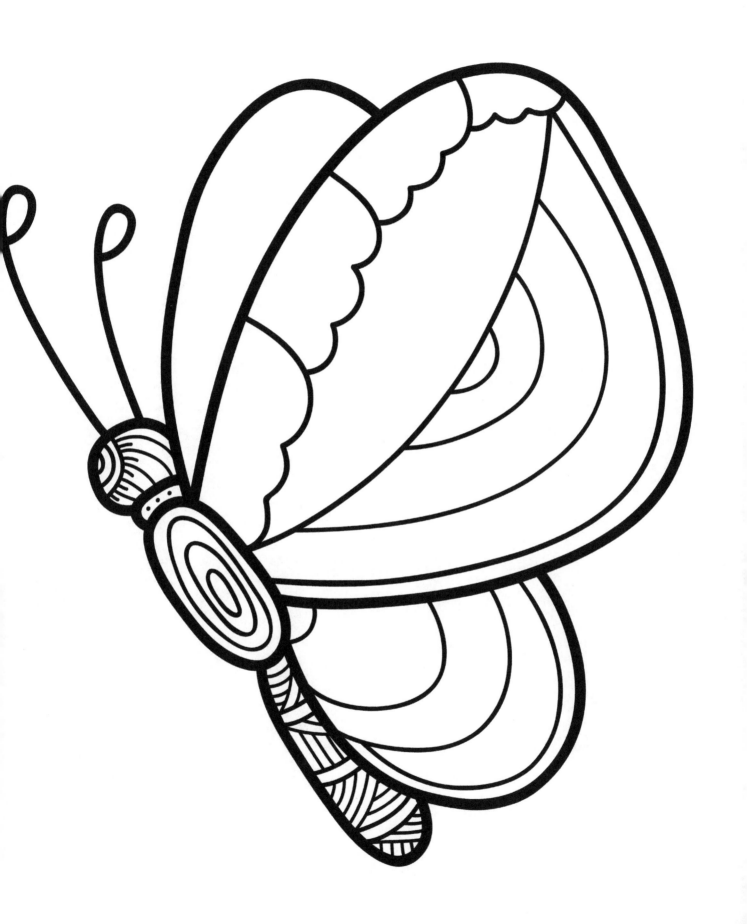

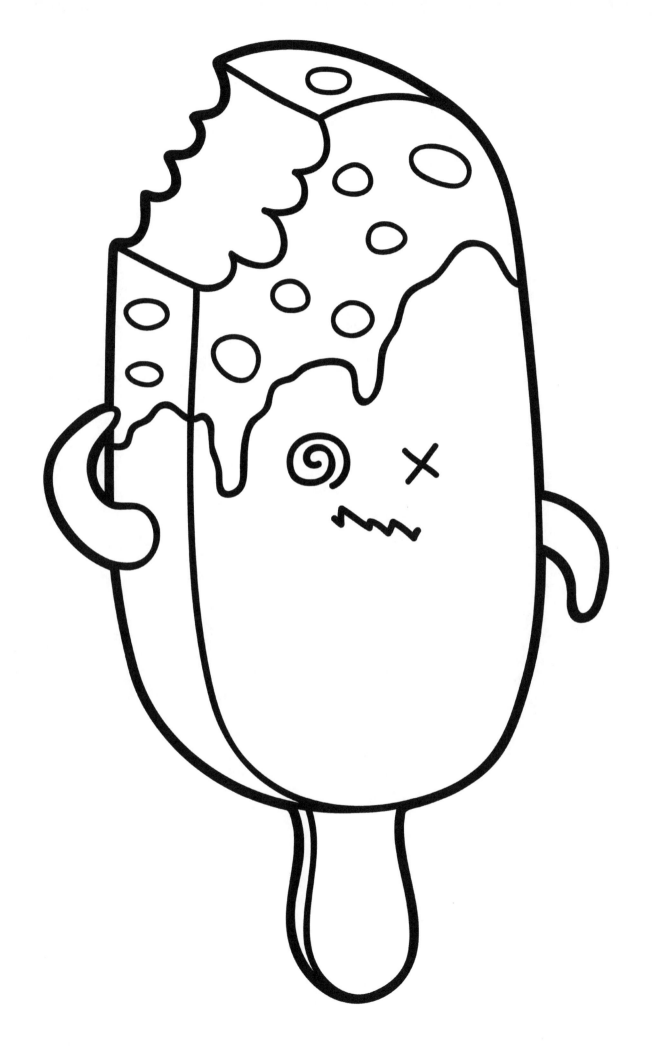

Bonus Pages

Turn the page for bonus pages from some of our most popular coloring and activity books.

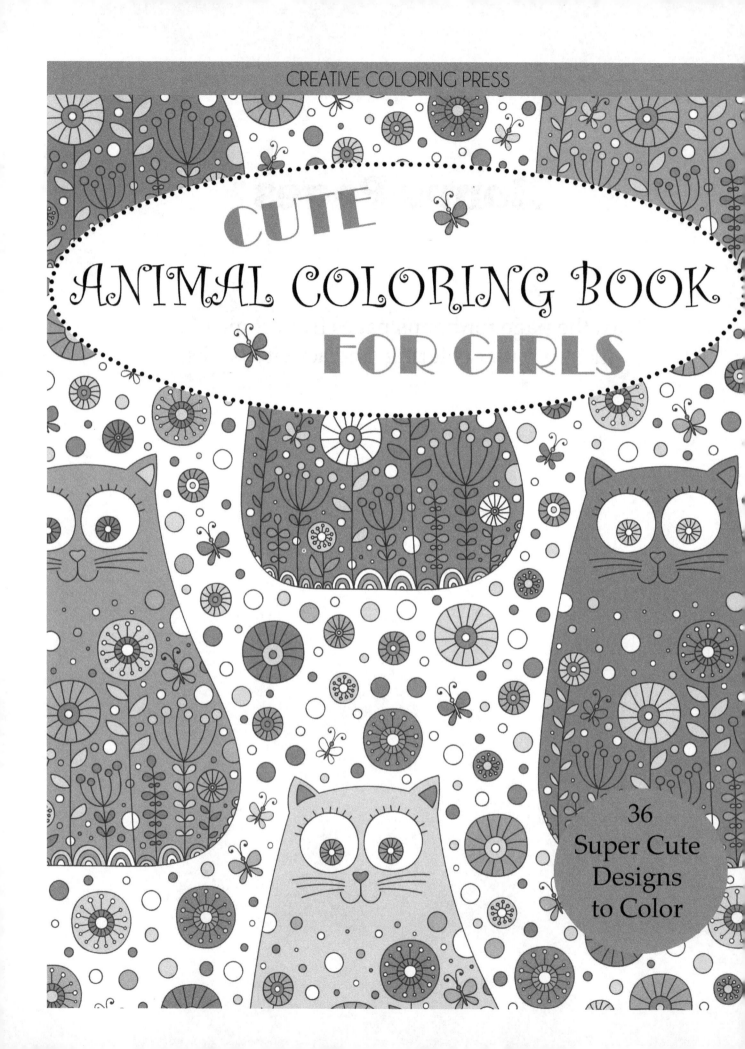

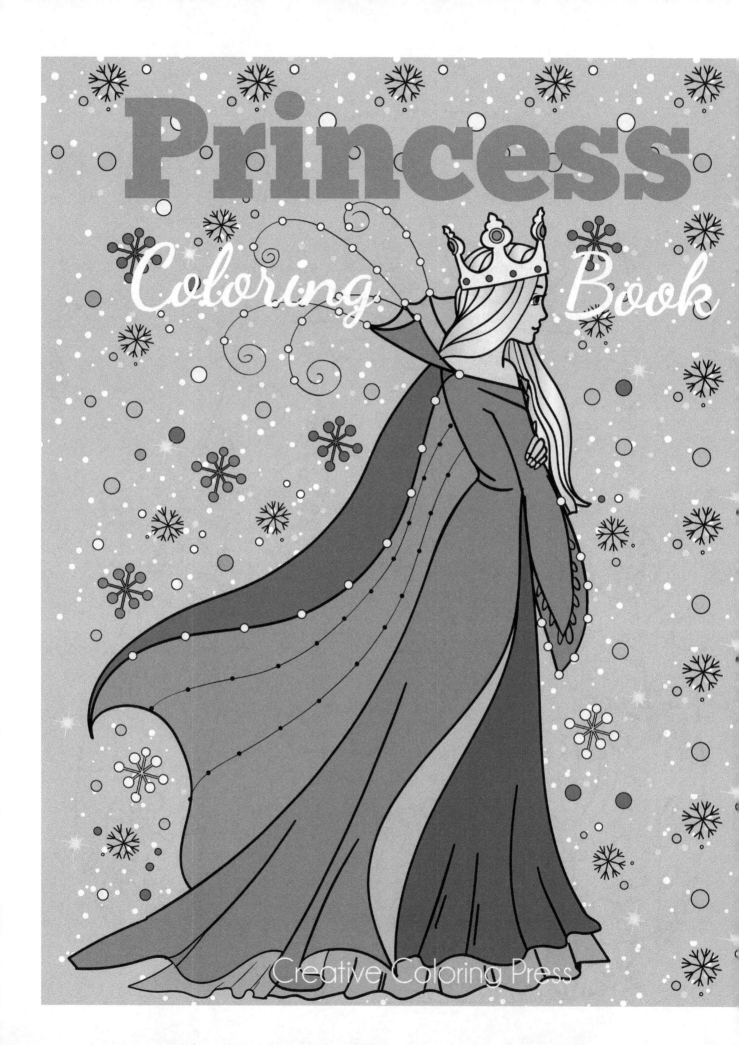

THINGS THAT GO
VEHICLE
COLORING
BOOK

BIG PRESCHOOL WORKBOOK

AGES 3-5

1.

2.

3.

4.

5.

LEARN LETTERS, NUMBERS, SHAPES, PATTERNS, AND MORE!

Trace & Color the Shapes

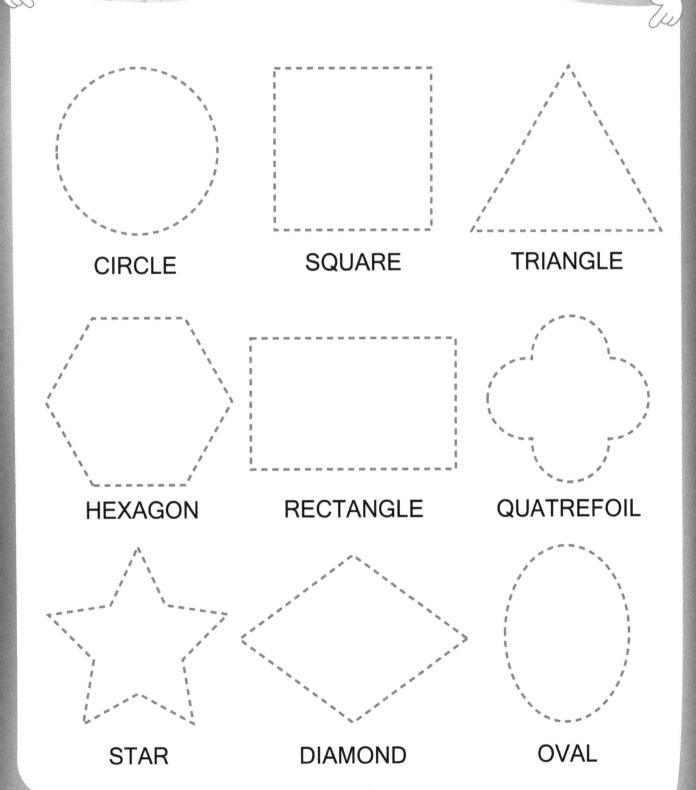

CIRCLE   SQUARE   TRIANGLE

HEXAGON   RECTANGLE   QUATREFOIL

STAR   DIAMOND   OVAL

CPSIA information can be obtained
at www.ICGtesting.com
Printed in the USA
LVHW062136281119
638900LV00016B/676/P